SACRAMENTO PUBLIC LIBRARY
828 "I" Street
Sacramento, CA   95814
1/10

D0554039

In Caesar's
Rome
with Cicero

In Caesar's
Rome
with Cicero

Text by Cristiana Leoni
Illustrations by Manuela Cappon

Marshall Cavendish
Benchmark
New York

This edition first published in 2009 in North America by Marshall Cavendish Benchmark.

Marshall Cavendish Benchmark
99 White Plains Road
Tarrytown, NY 10591
www.marshallcavendish.us

All rights reserved. No part of this book may be reproduced or utilized in any form or by any means electronic or mechanical, including photocopying, recording, or by any information storage and retrieval system, without permission from the copyright holder.

Copyright © 2003 Italian edition, Andrea Dué s.r.l., Florence, Italy

Library of Congress Cataloging-in-Publication Data

Leoni, Cristiana.
  In Caesar's Rome with Cicero / by Cristiana Leoni.
    p. cm. — (Come see my city)
  ISBN 978-0-7614-4328-5
  1. Rome—History—Republic, 265–30 B.C.—Juvenile literature. 2. Caesar, Julius—Juvenile literature. 3. Cicero, Marcus Tullius—Juvenile literature. 4. Rome—Social life and customs—Juvenile literature. 5. Rome—Politics and government—Juvenile literature. I. Title.
  DG254.L46 2009
  937'.6305–dc22

                              2008032316

Text: Cristiana Leoni
Translation: Erika Pauli
Illustrations: Manuela Cappon and Valeria Grimaldi

Photographs: pp. 6, 26, 42, 43 Scala Archives, Florence

Printed in Malaysia
1 3 5 6 4 2

Contents

Our Guide:

Marcus Tullius Cicero

Marcus Tullius Cicero was born into a wealthy family in Arpinum (in the region of Latium, not far from Rome) on January 3, 106 BCE. His father sent him to Rome to study law and Cicero became one of the best lawyers of his times. When he was twenty-six, in 80 BCE, he made a name for himself in a sensational trial. Cicero defended Sextus Roscius, who was charged with parricide (killing his father), and succeeded in proving that it was all a plot by the followers of the **dictator** Sulla to prevent Roscius from inheriting his father's estate. Fearing retaliation, Cicero went to Greece for two years, during which time Sulla died.

Upon his return Cicero actively took up his legal practice and began his political career. His first public office was that of *quaestor*, or administrator, of eastern Sicily for the year 75 BCE; he worked with integrity and youthful enthusiasm. As a result, a few years later the Sicilians asked Cicero to prosecute Gaius Verres, the governor who had robbed, defrauded, and misused his power. Cicero made violent orations against Verres and the conniving thief was forced into exile.

Cicero continued his career in politics, becoming a **consul** in 63 BCE. That year, **Catiline** (Lucius Sergius Catilina), an impoverished aristocrat, led a vast conspiracy to overthrow the Roman republic. Cicero discovered the conspiracy by chance and took immediate action. He denounced the plot in the senate, and all those involved who were captured in Rome were executed. Then, backed by a few legions, he went after Catiline's forces in **Etruria**. At the height of his political career, Cicero was proclaimed *Pater Patriae* (father of the country).

But Cicero made a serious mistake. Condemning the conspirators to death was illegal, for the law stated that no Roman citizen could be put to death until he had appealed to the people. So, in 58 BCE, Cicero's enemies sent him into exile. He was allowed to return eighteen months later and resume his legal practice in Rome.

Above: A marble bust of Cicero.

Facing page: A Roman patrician reading a wax tablet.

While Cicero was in exile, the struggle for power between Caesar and Pompey had begun. Cicero sided with Pompey, but avoided openly denouncing Caesar. He was named governor of the province of Cilicia in Asia Minor (today southern Turkey). When **civil war** broke out between the two leaders, Cicero realized that it was a struggle for the kingdom. Despite his lack of confidence and his uncertainty, he once more sided with Pompey. After Pompey's defeat, Cicero retired to **Brundisium** where he waited until he was sure of Caesar's pardon.

Back in Rome, Cicero led a private life. However, on March 15, 44 BCE, Caesar was assassinated in the senate and Brutus, holding up his bloody dagger, shouted "Cicero" in celebration of the regained liberty. Cicero then returned to politics and sided against Mark Antony, who proclaimed himself Caesar's heir despite the fact that the legal heir was Octavian. Cicero delivered fourteen impassioned orations against Antony. These speeches have come down in history as the *Philippics* (in memory of those the Greek orator **Demosthenes** pronounced against Philip II of Macedon).

Soon after Cicero's speeches, Octavian and Antony reconciled and made a pact, and Cicero tried in vain to flee to Greece by sea. Antony's henchmen caught up with Cicero in Formia, near Naples, where he had a villa on the coast. Cicero was executed on December 7, 43 BCE.

Map of the City

Originally a village of shepherds and farmers in the hills near a ford across the Tiber River, Rome grew to be the capital of an empire—a splendid, chaotic megalopolis with more than a million inhabitants.

When Cicero and Julius Caesar lived, approximately a hundred years before the birth of Christ, there was no Coliseum, no Trajan's Market, no Domus Aurea ("golden house"). But a temple to **Jupiter** stood on the Capitoline Hill and fierce chariot races were held in the Circus Maximus.

For centuries Rome was the hub of the Western world. People with different ideas and beliefs passed through the great city. The apostles Peter and Paul spread the teachings of Jesus Christ and were martyred in Rome. In fact, the pope is still headquartered in the Vatican City in Rome.

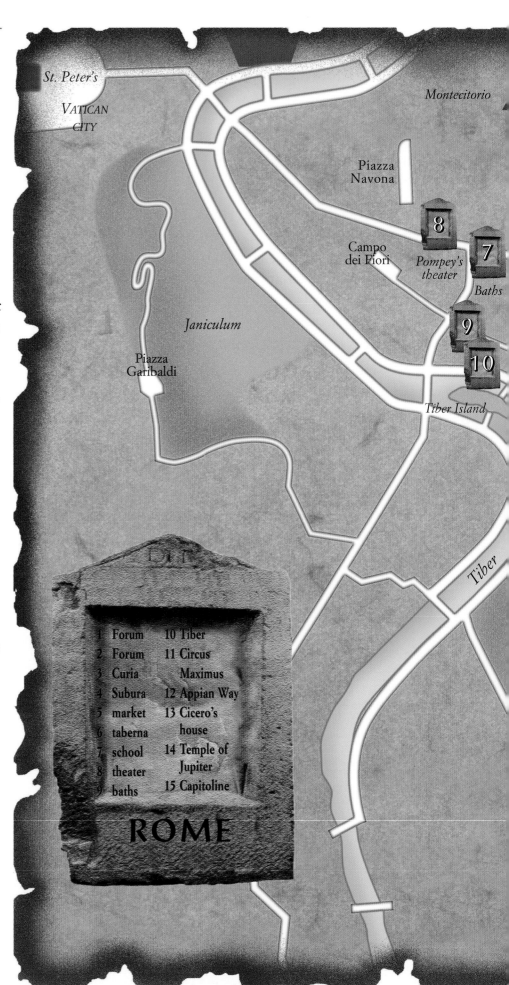

1	Forum	10	Tiber
2	Forum	11	Circus
3	Curia		Maximus
4	Subura	12	Appian Way
5	market	13	Cicero's
6	taberna		house
7	school	14	Temple of
8	theater		Jupiter
9	baths	15	Capitoline

ROME

Quirinal
Hill

6

S u b u r a

5

15

4

Trajan's
Market

Piazza del
Campidoglio

Temple of
Jupiter

Termini
Station

Via dei Fori Imperiali

14

3

Domus Aurea

Capitoline
Hill

2   1

13

Forums

Coliseum

Palatine
Hill

St. John
Lateran

Circus
Maximus

11   Porta Capena

Appian Way

Baths
of Caracalla

Appian Way

12

Park of
the Scipios

Porta
San Sebastiano

Rome!

It was our second day in Rome and we were atop the Janiculum, a hill overlooking Rome. My family had decided to go to Italy on vacation, which was a great choice: the hotel was nice, the weather was mild, and there weren't many tourists. My sister seemed excited—it was our first trip to Europe—and my parents were in a good mood. Things couldn't have been better. What a scatterbrain I am! I haven't introduced myself. My name is Anthony and I'm ten years old. I have a sister whose name is Julia. But let me tell you what happened to me a few months ago during our vacation in Rome. You won't believe it.

As I was saying, we were on the Janiculum taking in the panoramic view of the city. We couldn't believe our eyes. Two thousand years

Basilica of Santa Maria Maggiore

Torre delle Milizie (Tower of the Milices)

Il Gesù (Church of the Holy Name of Jesus)

Church of Sant'Andrea della Valle

ago Rome was the heart of a gigantic empire, and we were there gazing at an immense sea of roofs, monuments, churches, and domes stretching as far as the eye could see. It was a clear September morning and the houses and buildings seemed to glow against the blue sky.

While we were looking out over the city, trying to figure out what to do next, I felt as if someone were watching us. There wasn't anybody nearby, except for some tourists down at the other end who were busy taking pictures of each other. I couldn't shake

*Monument to
Victor Emanuel II*

*Church of
Santa Maria
in Aracoeli*

Capitoline

*Church of
San Carlo ai Catinari*

*Basilica of
St. John Lateran*

the feeling that two eyes hidden somewhere were following our every move. My parents didn't seem to notice a thing, but I felt strange. We decided to begin the day by visiting the Forum. A little white dog from the tour bus sat and waited as we studied the map. We began walking towards the bus stop and I turned around a couple of times to see if we were being followed, but there wasn't anybody there, except the little dog. I thought I caught a glimpse of somebody close behind us when we stopped at the newsstand to buy our tickets. But I was wrong again. As we boarded the bus, I told myself that I was being silly, shrugged my shoulders, and decided to forget it.

Strange Encounter at the Forum

Dad said that in antiquity the Roman Forum was a great square surrounded by the most important buildings in the city. Now all that's left is ruins, but it's still impressive. Julia especially liked the Temple of Vesta, which housed the city's sacred fire, while what struck me was the platform known as the Rostra. All that's left is a pile of stones, but I tried to imagine what it must have been like when the orators went up to speak to the people gathered in the square. Our guidebook says that the *rostra*, or prows, from enemy ships were put on the speakers' platform as trophies. Eventually the entire podium was called the Rostra. Then I looked at the stones in the pavement and thought of the thousands and thousands of feet that had passed over them in all these centuries! I began wondering what the ancient Romans were like. Were they tall or short? How did they live? It was time to move on and Mom and Dad were calling us, but Julia and I were lost in our daydreams.

And that's when it happened. Suddenly I had that same strange feeling I'd had at the Janiculum, but this time there was really someone there. A funny-looking man draped in a sheet was sitting on a nearby piece of column and watching us. The little dog was still with us and started to sniff at his feet, so we decided we could go closer, too.

Temple of Saturn

Rostra

"And who are you? May Jupiter strike me with a bolt of lightning if I ever saw clothes stranger than yours! Are you **Scythians**? No, I don't think so. Gauls? Do you belong to some people from far-off lands not yet under the domain of Rome? Speak up, strangers. Ah, I see. The sack you have on your back, my boy, tells me you are a servant. Tell me, little slaves, who is your master?"

columns of the Temple of Vespasian and Titus

remains of the Tabularium

1

An Exceptional Guide

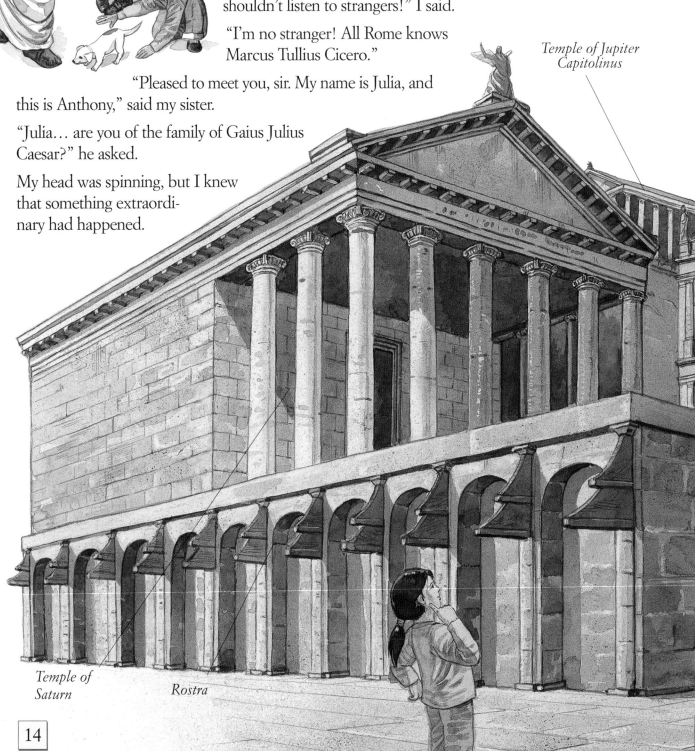

"I am not a slave and this is my little sister!" I answered him, somewhat taken aback.

"Then why aren't you wearing a toga the way any boy from a good Roman family does? And why does this little girl go around dressed like a boy, with Asian pants? Where's the servant who was supposed to take you safely to your tutor?"

"But school hasn't started yet! We're still on vacation! I'm sorry, sir, we can't talk with you. Mother says we shouldn't listen to strangers!" I said.

"I'm no stranger! All Rome knows Marcus Tullius Cicero."

"Pleased to meet you, sir. My name is Julia, and this is Anthony," said my sister.

"Julia… are you of the family of Gaius Julius Caesar?" he asked.

My head was spinning, but I knew that something extraordinary had happened.

Temple of Jupiter Capitolinus

Temple of Saturn

Rostra

The square looked different—we were in ancient Rome!

"Haven't you ever been in the Forum?" asked Cicero. "My dear children, this is the heart of Rome, seat of the political life, and meeting place for all."

"What's that building with all those columns, sir?" asked Julia.

"It's the Temple of **Saturn**. That's where the treasury of the Republic is kept."

"I want to know what that big building with the statues is!" I said.

"That is the Tabularium, where the state archives are stored. It was built about thirty years ago. The building in front of you is the Temple of Concord, founded by **Marcus Furius Camillus** to celebrate the end of the struggle between **patricians** and **plebeians**. It was here that I gave my speech against Catiline."

"What did she do that was so bad?" I asked.

"Catiline was a traitor, not a lady!" exclaimed Cicero, scandalized.

Temple of Concord

Tabularium

The Senate in Session

"Your servant seems to have been delayed, so you can come with me," said Cicero. "We'll send someone to look for him later. Well, then, no school you say? In that case, I'll see to your education today. I'm headed to the senate, which is also the best place to begin if you want to know about Rome. What province did you say you are from? Or are you relatives of Julius Caesar? No matter, it's not important. Let's go!"

As he said this Cicero took our hands and started off toward one of the buildings on the Forum. Once inside, I noticed that the people there were all draped in what looked like heavy, white sheets. After talking a minute with a funny-looking fat guy, all sweaty and puffing, Cicero returned with a satisfied look.

"A brief but important commitment," he said. "But now I am at your service! I see you're properly impressed by this solemn place—

it strikes awe into so many. This is the Curia, where the Roman Senate holds its sessions. These men, who decide on the most important questions of state, come from the best families and have held other important political offices before becoming senators."

"Mr. Cicero," interrupted Julia, pulling his clothing, "what are they doing?"

"They are preparing to speak. To take the floor you have to respect seniority; the oldest senators speak first, then the younger ones. The assemblies are presided over by a senator known as *princeps senatus*, or senate chief."

"And why are the senators dressed alike?" Julia asked. It occurred to me that my sister was beginning one of her series of questions on why and how—it could go on forever. I poked her in the ribs and put my finger to my lips.

"You should be asking more serious questions, little Julia," said Cicero sternly. "Senators wear white togas and those with purple borders are the highest magistrates."

He noticed our confused looks and exclaimed, "Don't you know what a toga is? For all the gods… Tell me, little Julia, what does your father wear? Doesn't he have a toga, or cloak, over his tunic?" We shook our heads. "What times we live in! I must say, it is practically impossible to understand the young people of today."

A Popular District

Cicero seemed to be a very important person. Someone was always stopping him as we walked down the streets. They asked for favors or offered him presents. Some people just nodded or winked at him, but others kept pestering him, complaining about their bad fortune and asking for his generosity. It seems we couldn't go three steps without someone coming up to Cicero.

"This way, children, up these stairs. We have to get away from these pests! The servants who usually come with me are off this morning—I'll never make that mistake again! How in the world could I have thought it possible to cross the *subura* without being bothered?"

"Look, Julia, you can see the whole street from here," I called to my sister from a balcony.

"Wow! Hey, look down there. Some lady is throwing garbage out the window!" she said.

"That's not unusual in the *subura*," said Cicero. "You've got to be careful when you walk in the street so you don't get hit by garbage or, even worse, the contents of a chamber pot. Julius Caesar tried to make all homeowners keep the space in front of their houses clean, but nobody pays attention to him. They're all tenants around here anyway."

"Look at the line for the fountain! Mr. Cicero, why are they all going to get water at the public fountain? Don't they have running water in their houses?" I asked.

Mr. Cicero started laughing. "What are you talking about? May the gods have mercy on us, these houses don't have running water, except maybe on the ground floor. We're in an *insula*—a city block—of a popular neighborhood. Those are the poor people who live in the upper stories of these houses. Only the wealthy are entitled to comforts and conveniences like running water and heating."

WATER IN ROME
When Cicero walked the streets in the first century BCE there were already four aqueducts that provided fresh water to Rome. Appius Claudius Caecus built the first, the Aqua Appia. Another seven were built over the next several hundred years, providing the city with the best supply of water in the ancient world. This enabled the *urb*s to become part of the central metropolis. Only recently have many cities succeeded in matching the capacity of the ancient Roman aqueducts. The Aqua Marcia, named after Quintus Marcus, still flows into some of the houses in Rome.

Shopping in Rome

I don't know how long our friend continued talking about the problems of the city: the chaotic traffic, lodgings, owners who were getting greedier, and tenants who were getting angrier. My sister and I had stopped listening. That's what happens when grown-ups start talking! The noise up ahead was getting louder and sounded lively, so we began walking faster (besides, Mr. Cicero had another appointment): it was a market.

"Stay close to me, children. Even in a small market like this, you never know when you might run into some untrustworthy character."

"Are there other markets in Rome?" asked Julia.

"Of course there are, young lady. There are many and each has its own specialty. If you need vegetables and beans you go to the *Forum Holitorium*. If you want pork you go to the *Forum Suarium*. I see you are particularly drawn to the donkeys. You'd find them in the *Forum Boarium*, although they deal mostly with cattle there."

It was fun listening to the cries of the vendors, even if I didn't understand a word. They acted just like the vendors back home at the farmers' market where my mother sometimes goes. The little dog felt right at home, too.

"Once there was a cobbler who attracted clients thanks to his talking crow," said Cicero. "A competitor, jealous of his success, stole the bird and hid it. But he hadn't counted on the reaction of the angry crowd, which practically tore him to bits!"

WARES FROM ALL OVER

Goods of all kinds flowed into Rome. Wheat came from Sicily and Egypt, pork from the Po Valley, and wine from Gaul and the Sabina region near Rome. Wool from Tarantum and Canosa in Apulia was in great demand.

There was also a lot of money coming in from the provinces and the newly conquered lands. There were money changers at nearly every street corner. They called out to people as if they were selling fruit or vegetables. Money changers could tell if a coin was authentic, and not counterfeit, by the sound it made when it was bounced off the counter or the street.

A Snack the Roman Way

Who would have thought that ancient Rome could be so noisy! We escaped the racket and the throngs of pedestrians crowding under a portico by slipping into a lane on the left.

"The gods save us from the crowd coming in for the free distribution of grain! The state distributes wheat to needy citizens for free. They have to be Roman citizens, male, and live in the **urbs**. Recently, however, Julius Caesar adopted a provision that reduced the number of those who were entitled to the dole. It's made him even less popular."

"Excuse me, sir, what time is it?" I asked after realizing my watch had stopped some hours earlier. All this talk about grain was making me hungry.

"I think it must be the eighth hour. Ah, of course. It does smell good, doesn't it? You must be hungry. Come on, let's have a bite in this *popina*."

The eighth hour, as I learned later, was 2:00 PM; the Romans started counting the hours of the day at 6:00 AM. As for the *popina*, it was kind of like an ancient fast-food place. However, I was so hungry it didn't matter much. I could smell grilled sausages and that was enough.

"Let's see," said our companion. "If I'm not mistaken they make an excellent spelt soup here. I think I'll have a bowl, and some hot mulled wine."

"We'll have some sausages and orangeade," I said after talking it over with Julia.

"I don't know what orangeade is. A sauce of some kind? In any case I suggest the sausages without sauce, and some water. You two look hot and thirsty."

The sausages were out of this world! And we gulped down the water. Even the little dog had found a bone to gnaw on.

FAST FOOD THE ROMAN WAY

In the noisy streets of Rome a *popina* offered people a quick snack, just like fast-food places today. The marble counter in a *popina* had large, round holes to hold terracotta jugs full of wine. Wine was served with either hot or cold water and could be spiced or sweetened with honey. The most famous wine in Italy was the Falerno, but only the rich could afford it. Less expensive wines came from Spain, Greece, and Gaul. Bread, sausages, olives, cheese, and eggs were served, and the customers ate their food right in the street.

Scuffles at School

Intrigued by the noise and shouting that came from a side street, we turned in to see what was going on. We soon came to a small, shabby building with a columned porch.

"That explains it all!" said our friend. "This is the school of Master Alcibiades! Scuffles are the norm here every day!"

The scene was actually quite familiar. There were about fifteen boys, more or less my age. A few were wrestling, some were running and jumping, and a couple of them were quietly minding their own business. In the midst of them the teacher, holding a cane, was trying in vain to calm things down. Julia and I hid behind a column to watch, but I wanted more than anything to join the fight.

"Mr. Cicero," I asked, "what subjects does this teacher teach?"

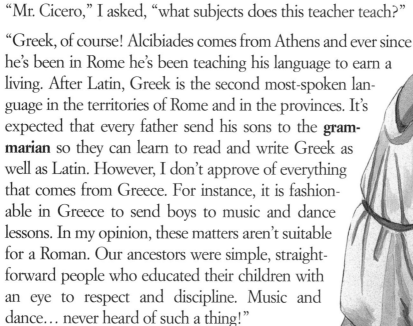

"Greek, of course! Alcibiades comes from Athens and ever since he's been in Rome he's been teaching his language to earn a living. After Latin, Greek is the second most-spoken language in the territories of Rome and in the provinces. It's expected that every father send his sons to the **grammarian** so they can learn to read and write Greek as well as Latin. However, I don't approve of everything that comes from Greece. For instance, it is fashionable in Greece to send boys to music and dance lessons. In my opinion, these matters aren't suitable for a Roman. Our ancestors were simple, straightforward people who educated their children with an eye to respect and discipline. Music and dance... never heard of such a thing!"

"What are those square boards the boys have?" I asked Cicero.

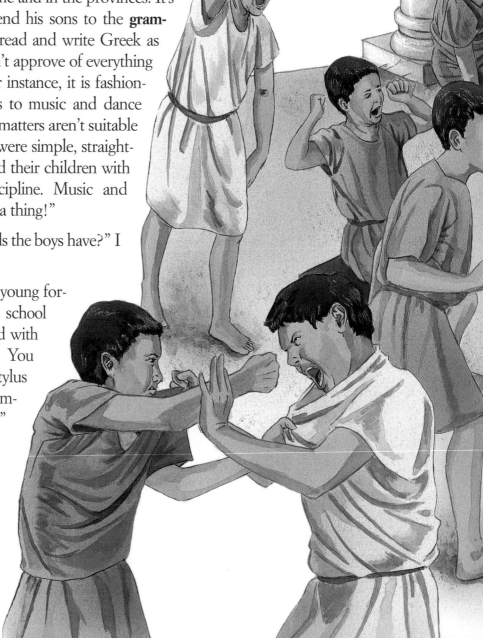

"You continue to amaze me, young foreigners. You said you go to school and yet you're not acquainted with the wax tablets for writing? You write in the wax with the stylus and when you're done you simply smooth out the wax again."

"Is that all you need to be a student?" I asked.

"Of course not," said Cicero, "you also need brains and discipline."

Above: Actors wore masks when they performed. There were both tragic masks (*left*) and comic masks (*right*).

Dress Rehearsal

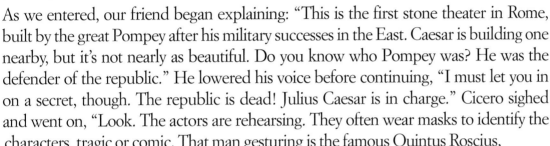

I had no idea how much time we had spent with Cicero, but Julia and I were getting tired.

"Mr. Cicero," my sister began to whimper, "my feet hurt!"

"Your upbringing is not what it should have been, I see. You haven't been properly educated. First of all, you must learn to endure pain. And secondly, where is your stamina? If we must slow down, we will, but that may mean there will not be time enough to see Pompey's theater, one of the marvels of Rome." Cicero kept walking as he scolded us. Julia and I looked at each other and decided we had better stop complaining and just follow him. After all, a theater was something special.

As we entered, our friend began explaining: "This is the first stone theater in Rome, built by the great Pompey after his military successes in the East. Caesar is building one nearby, but it's not nearly as beautiful. Do you know who Pompey was? He was the defender of the republic." He lowered his voice before continuing, "I must let you in on a secret, though. The republic is dead! Julius Caesar is in charge." Cicero sighed and went on, "Look. The actors are rehearsing. They often wear masks to identify the characters, tragic or comic. That man gesturing is the famous Quintus Roscius, who uses masks a lot. There'll be a full house today, not even standing room!"

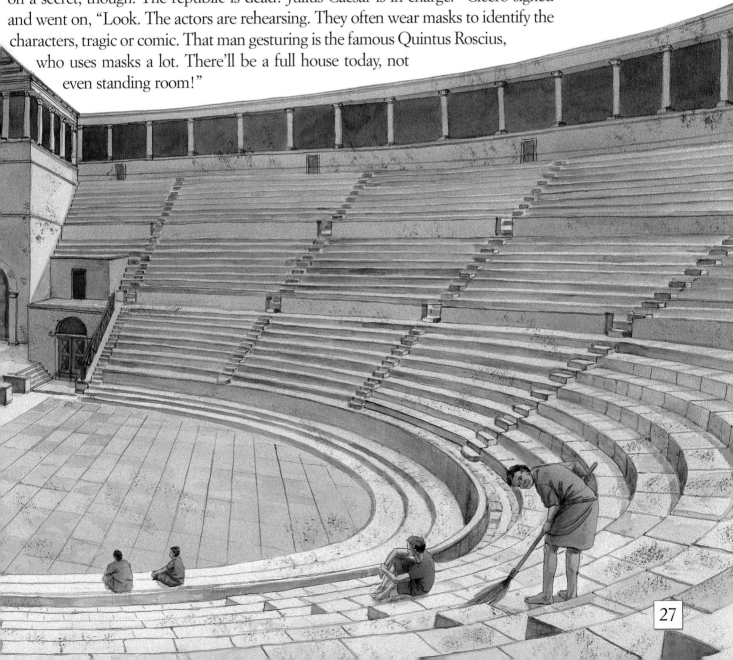

Hot and Cold Baths

What fun it was going around with Mr. Cicero! He knew about everything and never missed the chance to tell us. Although he seemed to think quite a lot of himself, he wasn't really all that stuck-up. He explained things clearly and slowly, and he was easy to understand.

As we were walking up a small street we heard the sound of a gong coming from a low building with a dome. It must have been a signal because a door opened to let in the people waiting on the sidewalk.

"I've got an idea!" said our friend, beaming. "If you're tired, why don't we go into the baths? It costs practically nothing and we can pause in a relaxing, comfortable place to get our energy back."

"Great idea! Is there a swimming pool, too?" I asked.

Cicero nodded, then gave the man at the entrance a friendly smile, and he let us in free.

"Come to think of it, we don't have time for more than a short visit. No use undressing! I still have to show you any number of things before evening! Let's sit down here a few minutes," said our guide as soon as we entered a small room were a few men were bathing in a round tub.

"This is the *frigidarium*. Here you bathe in cold water to invigorate the body. Normally people come here with a servant who helps them take care of their body. I come occasionally with my secretary. That way, while I am being massaged I can dictate a letter or he can take a few notes. First you go to the *tepidarium*, where the body gets used to the temperature change, then a hot bath in the *calidarium*, and, after another brief stop in the *tepidarium*, you come here to tone up your muscles with cold water."

I would have liked to take all those baths in hot, lukewarm, and cold water, but our guide was impatient to get on with our tour.

On the Banks of the Tiber

Our tour of Cicero's Rome continued through a district of narrow, winding streets lined with tall apartment buildings. As we rounded the last corner we saw the Tiber River. Right in the middle of the river was Tiber Island, which was where the sick went to be healed, according to Cicero. The city-side banks were obviously busy ports. There were boats everywhere, some waiting to dock while others were still tied to the pier. Men were unloading heavy bags and *amphorae*, shouting as each new load arrived at the docks. The whole place was in constant motion. Mr. Cicero took us down to the banks to a tranquil corner away from the incoming boats.

"What a great place, Mr. Cicero. Can we swim in the river?" Julia asked.

"I don't think that would be a good idea: the current is pretty strong and I can't dive in to rescue you. It wouldn't be very dignified, plus my toga is brand new. I've brought you here to show you one of the oldest places in Rome. Everybody knows that Romulus founded the city on the Palatine Hill, but my studies have convinced me that this is a key point in the origins of Rome. The ford is here and the road leading to Etruria is nearby, so merchants have been importing and exporting goods at this site for ages. As you can see, merchandise still arrives here from all over the world."

"I was hoping to see some big ships," I said, rather disappointed.

"The cargo ships that bring wheat to Rome from all the Mediterranean countries are too large to come this far. They stop at the port of Puteoli, in Campania, and unload their goods for land transport. Recently, however, the city of Ostia, at the mouth of the Tiber, has become more important as a commercial port. A few years will tell. In Ostia the wares are loaded onto those river boats, which are small, easy to handle, and can move against current.

"But how do they move upstream? Do they use oars?"

"Excellent question, my boy! They use neither oars nor sails; they are hauled up river by draft animals or slaves moving along the banks, using heavy ropes. See how many there are around here?"

Chariot Races

Imagine a sold-out crowd at a football stadium during the Super Bowl when the score is tied in the fourth quarter, and the result might be close to what happens at a chariot race in the Circus Maximus. First of all, the Circus Maximus was not like any circus I had ever seen; there was no tent, elephants, or clowns. This was just a gigantic race-track with stone bleachers.

"Well, what do you think?" asked Cicero.

"It's awesome! I've never seen anything like it!" I shouted. "Is this a big race?"

"Yes, it's one of the races of the *Ludi Magni*, which are held in honor of Jupiter Optimus Maximus."

"Why is he called Optimus Maximus?" I asked.

"Jupiter is the father of all the gods and we honor him as the best and greatest, or *optimus maximus*. In other words there's no

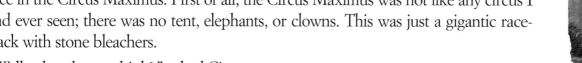

one above him. Let me explain how the races work. The chariot teams are organized into factions and distinguished by color. They have to complete seven laps. Right now they're in the second. See the markers?"

"What markers? Where?" I looked for a big display screen.

"Can't you see those eggs? Look at the man on the ladder: he has lowered the first egg and will lower the second as soon as they've finished this lap. Look, the first chariot is going into the curve! That's the hardest part: if the chariot is too close the driver risks hitting the edge of that long, low wall in the center and overturning, but if he is too far away he'll fall behind and maybe even lose control of his chariot. With a *quadriga* everything depends on the power and skill of the two horses running on the outside.

"What's the crowd shouting?" I asked.

"They are shouting the names of the charioteers. Everybody has a favorite, and usually one they really don't like, too. In the circus, charioteers are more important than senators or consuls."

The Queen of Roads

After the race we took a wagon outside the city walls. "One of the most important things in Rome is the Appian Way, the queen of all roads. Romans have built mile upon mile of roads, constructing bridges, leveling hills, and cutting through mountains. Our armies marched along these roads and spread Roman civilization to the far ends of the Earth! It is also thanks to roads like this that Rome, once a modest village of farmers and shepherds, is now the master of the known world."

Cicero paused as we looked around the countryside. He then started reciting the history of the Appian Way: "The Appian Way is named after the censor Appius Claudius Caecus, who had it built 260 years ago, but at the time it only went up to Capua. Afterward it was extended north to Brundisium and **Hydruntum**: in all, 410 miles (660 km) from Rome. It takes a normal traveler a couple of weeks to travel the whole way. It was originally built so the army could travel and get supplies quickly. Now, as you see, it's full of wagons transporting merchandise, travelers, messengers and, unfortunately, thieves. You have to be careful at night."

House without a Roof

We returned to Rome on a wagon that was taking wheat to the market. During the ride I noticed Cicero seemed worried. He had spent almost the entire day with us, forgot to tell his servants, and was afraid of what his wife, who apparently had a temper, would say.

We hurried on toward the Palatine Hill and an elegant residential district. Before going into his house, Mr. Cicero kicked the large wooden door a few times. "That's to keep away the evil eye," he said with a wink. "But please come in. Just make yourselves at home. Are you hungry? Or thirsty?"

"Tony," my sister interrupted, sounding alarmed, "Cicero's house doesn't have a roof!"

Our host burst out laughing. "You keep surprising me, little one. The opening you see is called an *impluvium*. It's there on purpose so that the rain water can be collected in the basin below to be used for domestic purposes. I even have running water and heating here!"

Cicero asked a servant where his wife was. She had decided to go visit some of her friends. After sending away the servant, who had documents for his master to read, Cicero gladly answered another of Julia's questions. "That tiny house in the corner is the altar to the gods of the house, to whom we make offerings every morning. There are the *lares*, spirits of our ancestors, and the *penates*, the guardians of the threshold." Then, almost whispering, he said, "That's also where we hide our precious objects and important documents. But, shhh, don't tell anyone."

The Temple on the Hill

After leaving Cicero's house we went down a long flight of steps and then up an even longer one. Our guide told us that it was called *Centum Gradus*, or "one hundred steps," but to us they felt like a thousand. At the top Cicero made fun of us because we were out of breath. I didn't have the strength left to be offended, and was panting too hard to answer. Once my heart slowed down I realized it was really worth it: there was a great square and a gigantic temple.

"Here we are on the Capitoline and what you're looking at is the Temple of Jupiter." began Cicero.

"Is it very old?" my sister asked.

"Not really. The old temple burned down almost forty years ago in a fire that destroyed the entire Capitoline. The original temple was built by the **Etruscan** kings **Tarquinius Priscus** and **Tarquinius Superbus**. As you know, many centuries ago Rome was governed by kings. At the time, the Etruscans, who lived to the north in Tuscia, were very powerful. They ruled the city for a time and built this temple, calling in their most famous artists to decorate it. Two other important goddesses, **Juno** and **Minerva**, were worshiped along with the father of the gods, Jupiter."

"There are a lot of people here," I noted.

"That's not always the case. Today is special because, as I already told you, this is when the *Ludi Magni* are celebrated. The celebrations last sixteen days; there are the chariot races at the Circus Maximus, a banquet in honor of the Capitoline divinities, and a great parade followed by the ritual sacrifice of a pig, a sheep, and a bull. Too bad we got here so late, people are already leaving."

A Change on the Capitoline

I was thirsty and opened my backpack to get out my water bottle. A sudden gust of wind blew some postcards out of my backpack and whirled them across the Piazza del Campidoglio. Julia and I ran after them. When we had retrieved them all we walked back to the spot where we left Cicero, but he wasn't there. In fact, it was as if we were in a completely different piazza. What happened to the temple and the Romans in togas? Instead we were surrounded by tourists dressed in jeans and sneakers. We were back in the twenty-first century! We could hear cars honking and the siren of an ambulance on the streets below. I glanced at my watch and, to my surprise, it was running again and said it was 9:45 AM. I didn't know what to think—had we imagined it all or had it really happened? I felt a hand on my shoulder: it was Dad!

"Come on, let's go. We'd better hurry or we won't have time to see the **Capitoline Museums**. Oh, there's your mother with the ice cream cones."

Despite my confusion, one look at the vanilla gelato with chocolate chips made me hungry. It tasted great and Julia and I happily ate it as we followed Mom and Dad.

15

Julius Caesar and His Times

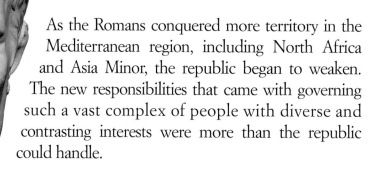

As the Romans conquered more territory in the Mediterranean region, including North Africa and Asia Minor, the republic began to weaken. The new responsibilities that came with governing such a vast complex of people with diverse and contrasting interests were more than the republic could handle.

Left: A marble bust of Julius Caesar.

Facing page, above: A nineteenth-century fresco depicts Cicero denouncing the Catiline conspiracy before the senate.

Facing page, below: Life in a Roman military camp.

During the second century BCE the Roman army was having difficulty recruiting soldiers, legislation limited the power of the upper class, and the political situation grew tense. The **Gracchi** brothers, well-connected and influential patricians, were advocates of plebeian causes, such as social equality. Each served as **tribune of the plebs**, Tiberius in 133 BCE and Gaius ten years later, and made enemies with the senate during their terms. They were accused of appealing to the plebs to increase their own power; Gaius, in particular, was self-serving. Both brothers were killed in the midst of political upheaval. The political situation disintegrated further in the next century with a civil war between Marius and Sulla, both popular military leaders. When Marius used bribery to defeat Sulla in a run for consulship, Sulla and his faction marched on Rome. Sulla was exiled, but returned in 83 BCE, seized control, and began his reign as dictator.

Barely ten years later, Catiline's conspiracy against the senate was exposed by Cicero. Then, generals Gaius Julius Caesar and Gnaeus Pompeius Magnus (Pompey) clashed in a new civil war. Caesar had conquered much of the west, while Pompey had freed the Mediterranean from pirates and added the provinces to Rome's territory. Caesar and Pompey were the most powerful men in Rome, and together with the richest man in Italy, Marcus Licinius Crassus, had made a pact known as the triumvirate.

The *triumviri* (or "three men") maneuvered the levers of political, financial, and military power in Rome. But when Crassus died, both Caesar and Pompey hoped to gain power and joined opposing political factions. Pompey was the defender of the senate and the patricians, Caesar (who could trace his family back to the origins of Rome) became the head of the powerful popular party.

The civil war ended in 48 BCE with Caesar's victory in Pharsalus; the senate was forced to give him perpetual dictatorship, the consulate, and even the office of **pontefix maximus**. He was also elected tribune, with no term limit, and his person became sacred and inviolable. He was the lord of an empire, a king without a crown. Caesar's reign ended on March 15, 44 BCE, when a group of conspirators, including some of his closest friends, stabbed him to death in the name of republican liberty.

However, Caesar's murder did not save the republic. A third civil war broke out in Rome as the conspirators, supported by the patricians under the leadership of Cicero, fought those loyal to Caesar, led by Mark Antony and the eighteen-year-old Octavian, Caesar's nephew and adopted son. Caesar's two heirs defeated their adversaries at Philippi in Greece, but then Mark Antony and Octavian turned against each other in a fight for power. Antony was defeated and, in 27 BCE, the senate conferred the title *augustus*—previously used only for the gods—to Octavian. An empire had been born at the expense of the republic.

Chronology

753 BCE – Romulus founds Rome on April 23.

753–509 BCE – Roman Kingdom. According to tradition, there was a succession of seven kings: Romulus, Numa Pompilius, Tullus Hostilius, Ancus Marcius, Tarquinius Priscus, Servius Tullius, and Tarquinius Superbus.

458 BCE – After defeating the Latins, Aequi, and Volsci, the Romans control Latium.

390 BCE – Brennus and the Gauls sack Rome.

272 BCE – The Romans defeat Pyrrhus, king of Epirus. They conquer Tarantum and southern Italy.

264–241 BCE – First Punic War against Carthage. Sicily becomes the first Roman province.

218–201 BCE – Second Punic War. Hannibal crosses the Alps and invades the peninsula but does not succeed in conquering Rome. On his return to Africa he is defeated by Scipio Africanus the Elder at Zama, in Tunisia.

210–208 BCE – Scipio Africanus the Elder takes many Spanish territories from Carthage.

200–190 BCE – Rome conquers northern Italy.

148 BCE – Greece becomes a Roman province.

146 BCE – Scipio Africanus the Younger (Scipio Aemilianus) destroys Carthage and puts an end to the Third Punic War. Rome controls the Mediterranean.

122–121 BCE – Tiberius and Gaius Gracchus attempt to impose a more just distribution of land conquered by the Roman army.

88–86 BCE – Civil war between Marius, backed by the *populares* (friends of the people), and Sulla, backed by the senate.

82 BCE – Sulla is dictator of Rome until 79 BCE.

73–71 BCE – The gladiator Spartacus rises against Rome with an army of gladiator slaves, but is defeated by Marcus Licinius Crassus.

63 BCE – Lucius Sergius Catalina conspires against the senate and is denounced by consul Marcus Tullius Cicero.

60 BCE – First triumvirate of Gaius Julius Caesar, Gnaeus Pompeius Magnus (Pompey the Great), and Crassus.

58–51 BCE – Caesar conquers land in western Europe.

49–46 BCE – Civil war between Caesar and Pompey. Caesar occupies Rome and Italy; Pompey and the senate flee to Greece.

48 BCE – Caesar defeats Pompey at Pharsalus in Greece. Ptolemy XII of Egypt has Pompey assassinated.

47 BCE – Caesar defeats the Egyptians on the Nile, near Alexandria, and puts Cleopatra on the throne of Egypt.

46 BCE – Caesar is nominated dictator for ten years.

44 BCE – Caesar is assassinated by conspirators in the senate. Mark Antony, Caesar's lieutenant, forces Brutus and Cassius out of Rome. Mark Antony claims power for himself, denying Octavian, Caesar's heir.

43 BCE – Cicero, who supports Octavian, speaks against Antony in the Senate. Octavian and Antony reach an agreement. Cicero is assassinated.

42 BCE – Battle of Philippi, in Thrace, where Octavian and Antony defeat the army of Brutus and Cassius. Mark Antony, who governs Egypt, marries Cleopatra.

31 BCE – Octavian defeats Mark Antony in the naval battle of Actium.

27 BCE – Octavian is named *Augustus Caesar* by the senate. His rule begins.

14 BCE–68 CE – The Julio-Claudian dynasty has imperial power. Tiberius, Caligula, Claudius, and Nero serve as emperors.

ca. 30 CE – Jesus Christ is crucified in Judea. Six million Roman citizens live in the territories ruled by Rome.

64 – Nero sets fire to Rome. The first persecution against Christians in Rome; apostles Peter and Paul are among the victims.

79 – Vesuvius erupts and destroys Pompeii, Herculaneum, and Stabiae.

98–117 – Under the emperorship of Trajan, the territory ruled by Rome reaches its maximum.

249–151 – First general persecution of the Christians.

260–268 – The empire is attacked by the Franks, Alemanni, Goths, and Parthians.

284–305 – Reign of Diocletian. A constitutional reform introduces the tetrarchy (rule of four) composed of two augusti and two caesars.

313 – Constantine issues the Edict of Milan, which extends freedom of worship to all religions.

324–337 – Constantine abolishes the tetrarchy and becomes the sole emperor. The capital is transferred to Constantinople (ancient Byzantium).

379–385 – Reign of Theodosius the Great. The Edict of Thessalonica makes Christianity the official religion of the empire.

395 – Theodosius dies and the Roman Empire is divided into the Eastern Roman Empire and the Western Roman Empire.

410 – Visigoths led by Alaric sack Rome.

452 – Pope Leo I convinces Attila, chief of the Huns, to abandon Italy.

476 – The barbarian king Odoacer deposes emperor Romulus Augustus, marking the end of the Roman Empire in the west (Byzantium, the eastern empire, remains until 1453).

Glossary

Brundisium, Adriatic port, today Brindisi (in Apulia).

Camillus, Marcus Furius, the Roman general who conquered the Etruscan city of Veii in 396 BCE.

Capitoline Museums, museum that houses the oldest public collections of Roman artifacts and monuments, including sculpture from ruins of Roman baths, basilicas, houses, and gardens.

Catiline (Latin: Lucius Sergius Catilina), the leader of a conspiracy against the republic. His plot was uncovered by Cicero.

civil war, a war fought by opposing factions belonging to the same state. In ancient Rome the first civil war (88-82 BCE) broke out between the followers of Marius and those of Sulla. Other civil wars were fought between Julius Caesar and Pompey (49-48 BCE) and Mark Antony and Octavian (32-30 BCE).

consul, the highest magistrate in the Roman Republic. There were always two elected for one-year terms.

Demosthenes, (384-322 BCE), Athenian statesman and orator who defended the liberty of Greece against the ambitions of Philip II of Macedon.

dictator, a political office in the Roman Republic that was above the three constitutional branches of government, so his power went unchecked. A dictator was appointed in serious circumstances, commanded the army, and could stat in office no longer than six months.

Etruria, the region north of Rome that was inhabited by the Etruscans (present-day Tuscany).

Etruscans, an ancient people who established the first great civilization in central Italy (7th–4th centuries BCE). They had artistic, religious, and social influence on the Romans, who overpowered them in 265 BCE. The last three of the legendary Kings of Rome were Etruscans.

Gracchi, the brothers Tiberius (163–133 BCE) and Gaius (154–121 BCE), both tribunes of the plebs. They sponsored agrarian reforms that inspired the peasant masses rise up against the nobles and the Roman gentry, which owned large agricultural estates (*latifundia*). They were both killed after the uprisings.

grammarian, schoolteacher in ancient Rome who taught reading and writing.

Hydruntum, Adriatic port, today Otranto (in Apulia).

Juno, (Gk. Hera) female counterpart to and consort of Jupiter. She was the goddess of the female principle of life and the most important of the Roman goddesses.

Jupiter, (Gk. Zeus) the highest Roman divinity, lord of all the gods.

Marcus Aurelius, (121–180 CE) Roman emperor; his equestrian statue, the only example of a unique style of Roman sculpture, was in the center of the Piazza del Campidoglio (now replaced by a copy).

Minerva, (Gk. Athena) the Roman goddess of wisdom, the arts, and war.

Octavian, (63 BCE–14 CE) the first Roman emperor, better known by his title, Augustus.

patricians, members of the families whose heads were senators (*patres*). In Caesar's time the name was extended to all nobles.

plebeians (plebs), members of the lowest social class of ancient Rome. The plebeians eventually succeeded in gaining recognition of their political and civil rights.

pontefix maximus, the president of the college of priests. The college consisted of common citizens who oversaw public worship and the morality of the Romans.

quadriga, a four-horse racing chariot.

Saturn, the Roman god of agriculture and harvest.

Scythians, an ancient people who lived in the region of Ukraine and who came into contact with Rome in the lands around the Black Sea.

subura, the proletarian district of Rome. Most were crowded, noisy, and dirty.

Tarquinius Priscus (Tarquin the Elder), Etruscan who was the fifth king of Rome (died ca. 579 BCE).

Tarquinius Superbus (Tarquin the Proud), Etruscan who was the seventh and last king of Rome (534–510 BCE). He was ousted by a patrician revolt in 506 BCE, marking the beginning of the Republic in Rome.

tribune of the plebs, elected magistrate who represented the plebeians. Two served at a time, and each was sacred and inviolable and had the right to defend the plebs regardless of decisions rendered by the senate.

urbs, Latin for "city." The Romans used to call their capital—Rome—simply "urbs," or "the city."

Index

Page numbers in **boldface** are illustrations, tables, and charts.